Building Victorious Faith

Part 1

Milton Whitley, Jr.

For information regarding permission or additional copies, contact publisher:

Knowledge Power Books
25379 Wayne Mills Place, Suite 131
Valencia, CA 91355
www.knowledgepowerbooks.com
661-513-0308

ISBN: 978-0-9888644-9-8
Library of Congress Control Number: 2013946629
Editor: Dolly Ogawa Amst
Graphic Design: John Sibley, Rock Solid Productions
Interior Layout: John Sibley, Rock Solid Productions

All Scripture quotations are from the King James Version of the Holy Bible.

Printed in the United States of America

Dedication

This book is dedicated to the precious memory of my mother. My mother was the first person to introduce and teach me about the tender, loving, mercy of God's eternal goodness. It was also my mother who first told me that God loved me so much, that He sent His Only Begotten Son, to die on the cross just for me. I can still recall my mother saying, "son, study God's Word, have faith in God's Word, and always, always, pray."

Mamma, thank you.

I Love You!

Special Thanks

I would like to give thanks to the entire staff at Knowledge Power Communications for believing in me, working so patiently with me and for affording me the opportunity to complete this project. There is also another personal spotlight of recognition that I would like to give to various family members, co-workers, and friends who believed in me over the years, allowing themselves to be multiple sources of priceless constructive feedback.

Thank you so much for your continuous words of inspiration, motivation and encouragement. You have truly enriched my life.

Much love and many, many thanks.

Acknowledgment

Titus 1:2
*In hope of eternal life, which God, that cannot lie,
promised before the world began;*

Romans 10:17
*So then faith cometh by hearing,
and hearing by the word of God.*

Hebrews 11: 1-3
*Now faith is the substance of things hoped for, the
evidence of things not seen.*

CONTENTS

Building Victorious Faith

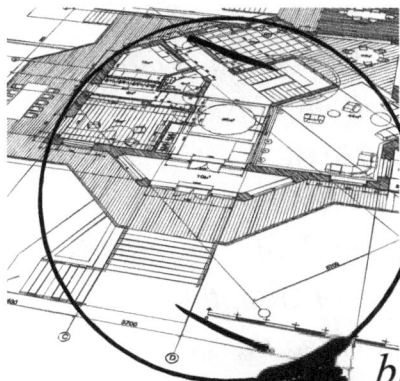

Diligently seek to study the blueprints of God's Eternal Word

First, you must have:

Plan – Discover God's promises found in His Word.

Design – Discover what's God's design for your life.

Blueprint – Identify all of the restrictions, conditions, and requirements found within the blueprint.

Look upon mine afflictions and my pain;
and forgive all my sins.
Psalms 25:18

When Jesus heard that, he said, this sickness is not
unto death, but for the glory of God, that the Son of
God might be glorified thereby.
Matthew 6:12

Who forgiveth all thine inquities;
who healeth all thine diseases;
Psalms 103:3

For thou, Lord, art good, and ready to forgive; and
plenteous in mercy unto all them that call upon thee.
Psalms 86:5

Forgive

Sometimes in the stillness of the night, countless thoughts of bitterness from the past, attempt to over flow and invade the sacred banks of my soul, that contain endless supplies of God's eternal loving, forgiving grace.

I am reminded, that if God can forgive me, I must and can also forgive others.

It's God's love and forgiveness, abiding deep within my redeemed spirit that flows continually down stream, divinely cleaning, purifying, and reconstructing the old sinful man.

Only God's loving, grace can change into something brand new, that which was once old, broken, and discarded by the world.

As God's divine river of love begin to flow through one's life, it will start to remove the hurt, sickness, and the pain of sin, for a final deposit into a very special place called,
"the sea of eternal forgetfulness."

Milton Whitley, Jr.

Finally be strong in the Lord,
and in the strength of his might.
Ephesians 6:10

Order my steps in thy word: and let not any iniquity
have dominion over me.
Psalms 119:133

Wherefore let them that suffer according to the will
of God commit the keeping of their soul to a faithful
Creator in doing what is right.
1 Peter 4:19
(NASB)

Strength

With the strength and boldness of a young lion, having total confidence in the power, love, mercy and goodness of the God to whom I serve, I boldly declare, that "I can do all things through Christ Jesus, who strengthens me."

When the Lord ascended into glory he instructed his followers to wait, for the promised Spirit of Truth, who when appeared would endow or baptize them with power.

Through the indwelling of the Holy Spirit and the importation of His power, we being many individuals, coming together, as a collective body of members within the body of Christ Jesus, possess all of the strength or power we need, to truly witness to a hungry world.

We are admonished to remember, that the joy of the Lord is our strength.

*But there is a spirit in man: and the inspiration of
the Almighty giveth them understanding.*
Job 32:8

*All scripture is given by inspiration of God, and is
profitable for doctrine, for reproof, for correction,
for instruction in righteousness;*
2 Timothy 3:16

*Happy is the man that findeth wisdom, and the man
that getteth understanding.*
Proverbs 3:13

*The fear of the Lord is the beginning of knowledge:
but fools despise wisdom and instruction.*
Proverbs 1:7

Inspirational

It can be a mind blowing experience trying to grasp from a mere mortal's point of view, an understanding of the depth and width of God's eternal love for humanity.

It is therefore by faith, that I don't have to comprehend it. I only have to accept it as a divine gift from a loving Father.

It's quite inspiring to realize, that the same God, who created both the heavens and the earth, by speaking them into existence, gave each star a specific name.

This same creative, all powerful God, also knew me, and called me by name before the foundations of the world was even formed.

It's truly an awesome experience just to be called a child of God and a joint heir with Christ Jesus, who has endowed me with power from on high, through the indwelling of the Holy Spirit.

Building Victorious Faith

*Carefully select the appropriate construction site
and all necessary materials needed
for continuous building, despite
unwarranted attacks or other intentionally
created distractions.*

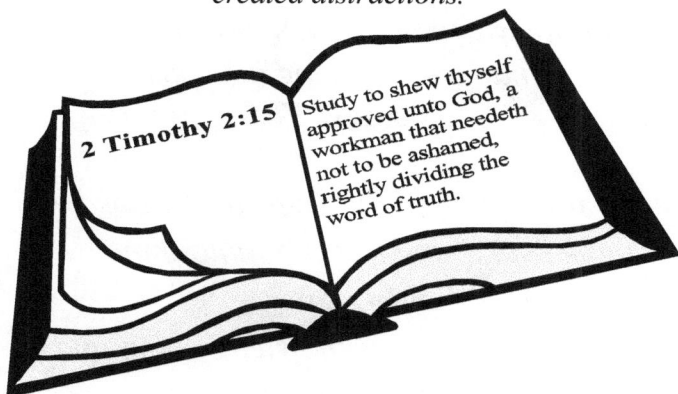

2 Timothy 2:15 Study to shew thyself approved unto God, a workman that needeth not to be ashamed, rightly dividing the word of truth.

Second, you've got to prepare:

Gather all of the materials required for continuous construction

Have the necessary defensive armor readily available to withstand any prolong attack from the enemy

Prepare a sound foundation for your project through prayer, meditation, and study of God's World

Securely store in the treasure chest of the heart what the Word says and doubt not.

*Commit thy works unto the Lord, and thy thoughts
shall be established.*
Proverbs 16:3

*Commit thy way unto the Lord; trust also in him;
and he shall bring it to pass.*
Psalms 37:5

*Commit thy way unto the Trust in the Lord with all
thine heart; and lean not unto thine own
understanding.*
*In all thy ways acknowledge him, and
he shall direct thy path.*
Proverbs 3: 5-6

*Wherefore let them that suffer according to the will
of God commit the keeping of their soul to a faithful
Creator in doing what is right.*
1 Peter 4:19

Commitment

I stand firmly and boldly, on the mountain top
of the present, grinning from ear to ear..

While peering through the smoky lenses of this
limited telescope called time.

As it was foretold by the prophets, concerning the
Word of God, that would become flesh and
dwell among sinful men.

I see the Living Word, being totally committed
to completing the will of His Father.

Looking through the clouds of His mercy,
I also see the blood that was shed, because of
man's fall from grace.

I'm grateful for God's commitment towards
humanity concerning His gifts of infinite
love and eternal life.

Now faith is the substance of things hoped for, the evidence of things not seen.
Hebrews 11:1

But without faith it is impossible to please him; for he that cometh to God must believe that he is a rewarder of them that diligently seek him.
Hebrews 11:6

By faith Moses, when he was born, was hid three months of his parents, because they say he was a proper child; they were not afraid of the king's commandment.
Hebrews 11:23

Knowing this, that the trying of your faith worketh patience.
James 1:3

Faith / Faithful

Although I am surrounded on every side
by enemies and the darkness of the this world,
I will not live in fear or be fearful.

Through faith in Christ Jesus,
the only true light in this world,
is there hope for producing enough illumination,
as guidance for the feet, while at the same time,
highlighting the directions to the divine path, which
leads to that final celestial destination of peace and
rest for the soul.

When I have faith and belief in Christ,
the Holy Spirit will lead, guide and protect me
from all hurt, harm or danger.

With your hand, held firmly and securely by Jesus,
the Holy Spirit will see you through
all trials, or tribulations.

Christ, is faithful, and will one day,
permanently defeat that last and final enemy
called "Death."

For God has not given us a spirit of fear, but of power and love and a sound mind.
2 Timothy 1:7

Thou shalt not be afraid for the terror by night; nor for the arrow that flieth by day. Nor for the pestilence that walketh in darkness; nor for the destruction that wasteth at noonday.
Psalms 91:5-6

Peace I leave with you, my peace I give unto you: Not as the world giveth, give I unto you. Let not your heart be troubled, neither let it be afraid.
John 14:27

The secret of the Lord is with them that fear him; and he will shew them his covenant.
Psalm 25:14

Fear/Fearful

When I think about the grace,
goodness and the mercy of God, why should I live
in fear or be fearful concerning anything in this life.

If I accept Jesus Christ as Lord and
Savior of my life, then what need do I have to be
fearful, concerning what may or may not happen.

The Word says, God is faithful and
cannot lie, whatever He promises,
He will bring it into fulfillment.

God is the only true friend that will never forsake
you, so chose this day to refuse to be a bond servant
to fear and doubt in any form.

Calling those things that be not,
as though they were, cast all fear and fearful
thoughts into the river of forgetfulness.

You are the head,
not the tail, you're a King's kids, in Christ,
you have the divine favor of God.

O Lord God in thee do I put my trust: save me from them that persecute me, and deliver me.
Psalms 7:1

My times are in thy hand: deliver me from the hand of mine enemies, and from them that persecute me.
Psalms 31:15

Thy mercy, O Lord, is the heavens; and thy faithfulness reacheth unto the clouds.
Psalms 35:6

All thy commandments are faithful: they persecute me wrongfully; help thou me.
Psalms 119:86

Persecution

Lately it appears that I and those connected to me,
have come under some sort of attack.

These attacks seems to be coming from every
possible side, by the forces of the enemy,
or at least from some of his officially
licensed representatives.

The enemy has tried to destroy my ability to drive,
my health, and even has encouraged the
destruction of my personal property.
It appears that I have been placed right in the center
of the cross hairs of the enemy's artillery for attack.

I've therefore, decided, being firmly convinced not
to worry or stress, but claim the victory that's found
in the blood of Christ, by standing on and speaking
boldly God's unchangeable Word.

Building Victorious Faith

Remember that the purchase price required as a down payment for the construction permit and rights to redeem your eternal soul was paid in full by the death, burial, and resurrection by our Lord and Savior Jesus Christ on the

Third, organize your construction process.

Faith comes by hearing, and hearing by the Word of God.

Call those things that be not as though they were. Speak to the mountains in your life.

Do not be double minded in your thinking and your speech.

Do not be moved by what you see, hear or feel.

Develop a daily habit to devote time to study of the Word, meditation and prayer for strength.

For whatsoever things were written aforetime were written for our learning, that we through patience and comfort of the scripture might have hope.
Romans 15:4

For the hope which is laid up for you in heaven, whereof ye heard before in the word of the truth of the gospel.
Colossians 1:5

And God shall wipe away all tears from their eyes; and there shall be no more death, neither shall there be any more pain: for the former things are passed away.
Revelation 21:4

They that fear thee will be glad when they see me; because I have hoped in thy word.
Psalms 119:74

Hope

At the end of the day, I lay my head down on my
pillow in victory. I rest in the confidence and
knowledge of just what God, through His Son, Jesus
has truly done for me.

It is through the shaded blood of Christ on Calvary,
That I am forgiven of all my sins and at the same
time redeemed for the promise in hope of enjoying
eternal life of paradise.

My victory of hope lay, in the promises made by an
all seeing, all knowing, and all powerful,
Eternal God.

The great I AM, who cannot lie, speaks calling
things that be not as though they were.

The power of His Word created of both
the heavens and the earth.

Having unshakable faith in the power of this same
Word (The Great I AM), sustains my hope.

Milton Whitley, Jr.

*Let the words of my mouth and the meditation of my
heart, be acceptable in thy sight,
O Lord, my strength, and my redeemer.*
Psalms 19:14

*There is no speech nor language,
where their voice is not heard.*
Psalms 19:3

*My meditation of him shall be sweet:
I will be glad in the Lord.*
Psalms 104:34

*My mouth shall speak of wisdom; and the meditation
of my heart shall be of understanding.*
Psalms 49:3

Meditation

Meditating on the goodness of God produces
continued sources of renewable grace,
strength and wisdom.

When I meditate on the grace and goodness of God,
I've provided the vital foods necessary for the
survival and development of the spirit man that live
within this old mortal house of clay.

When I meditate on the things of God, its becomes
easier to develop a Christ like mind, thus becoming
more in tuned with the will of the Spirit of God.

When I meditate on the things of God, I can expect
to receive power through the Holy Spirit to
overcome the forces of fear, to be at peace and to
maintain the soundness of mind.

And when I meditate in the spirit seeking guidance,
my spirit, communicates directly with the Holy
Spirit, who abides within each believer.

Milton Whitley, Jr.

Blessed is the man that endureth temptation: for when he is tried, he shall receive a crown of life, which the Lord hath promised to them that love him.
James 1:12

The Lord knoweth how to deliver the godly out of temptation, and reserve the unjust unto the day of judgment to be punished.
2 Peter 2:9

And lead us not into temptation, but deliver us from evil: for thine is the kingdom, and the power, and the glory, forever. Amen
Matthew 6:13

Watch and pray, that ye enter not into temptation: the spirit is indeed willing, but the flesh is weak.
Matthew 26:41

Temptation

Applying the spiritual mental brakes, attempting desperately to block and control the avalanche of unsolicited thoughts trying to successfully gain entry to the sacred sanctuary of my eternal soul.

Thoughts too numerous to even began to count, or to write on this single sheet of paper, flow like a mighty river alone a reinforced levees of scriptural resistance, in search a single point of weakness.

The royal guards of my spirit, continuously meditates on the word, and have been given the ultimate responsibility, of guarding against and preventing all kinds of possible breaches, within the spiritual sanctuary of the spirit.

The routine daily duties and orders for a true royal guard, during any given hour of the day, is to simply resist, and deny entry of any kind, to any and all potential enemies of the soul.

Building Victorious Faith

When Christ Jesus died on the cross, he took the keys of power over death, hell, and the grave from the devil. It was through the death, burial and the resurrection of our Lord and Savior, that as believers, we also now have access to the only key, that unlocks the only door containing the mercy and goodness of God that leads to eternal life.

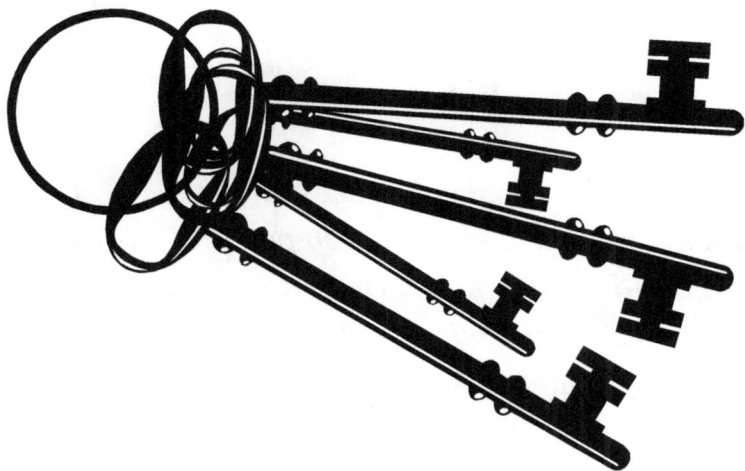

Fourth, the Move-in:

When the things that you have been believing for comes to pass, you've just been given the keys to experience the reality of God's mercy and goodness, as displayed through the fulfillment of the blessing.

I will both lay me down in peace, and sleep: for thou, Lord, only makes me dwell in safety.
Psalms 4:8

The Lord will give strength unto his people; the Lord will bless his people with peace.
Psalms 29:11

For he is our peace, who hath made both one, and hath broken down the middle wall of partition between us.
Ephesians 2:14

The Lord is my shepherd; I shall not want. He maketh me to lie down in green pastures; he leadeth me besides still waters. He restoreth my soul: he leadeth me in the path of righteousness for his name sake. Yea, though I walk through the valley of death, I will fear no evil: for thou art with me; thy rod and thy staff they comfort me. Thou prepares a table before me in the presence of mine enemies: thou anointest my head with oil; my cup runneth over. Surely goodness and mercy shall follow me all the days of my life: and I will dwell in the house of the Lord for ever.
Psalms 23

Peace

If it were not for the shed blood, of Jesus on the
cross placed in the hollow grounds on a hill called
"Calvary," there would have never been any peace
or rest, for my eternal soul, only war
and everlasting damnation.

If it were not for the love of God, and his
foreknowledge, which occurred eons before the
creative plan even began,
I would have been forever lost.

But through God's grace, He formulated a plan of
redemption, in order to save countless loss sinners
just like me.

If it were not for God's love, his mercy and his
grace, there could have never been the even remote
possibility for hope.

The peace of God, the true God kind of peace,
goes far beyond all physical and natural sources
connected to the knowledge of this world.

O Lord my God, I cried unto thee,
and thou hast healed me.
Psalms 30:2

The Lord upholdeth all that fall, and raiseth up all
those that be bowed down.
Psalms 145:14

Who forgiveth all thine iniquities;
who healed all thine diseases;
Psalms 103:3

The Lord will sustain him upon his bed:
In his illness, thou dost restore him to health.
Psalms 41:3
(NASB)

Health

Prolong imprisonment by countless moments of solitude, often reveals old painful and memories.

Old memories, like leaves that studiedly fall from a series of large trees, nestled together, mark the end of long summer days and the beginning onslaught of silence, brought on by the harsh coldness of equally long winter nights.

Reflecting back to special moments in time, reminiscing, desperately attempting to retain, if but for only a few brief precious seconds, we desperately grasp at any quickly fleeting shadows of vanity representing, "our health, our wealth and our youth."

What will be...always was...and what was... will always be.

Any photo from yesterday, compared with what you now see, is revealed in that mirror of truth, we grudgingly called, "Today."

Then he said unto him, go your way, eat the fat, and drink the sweet, and send portions unto them for whom nothing is prepared: for this day is holy unto the Lord: neither be ye sorry; for the joy of the Lord is your strength.
Nehemiah 8:10

They that sow in tears shall reap in joy.
Psalms 126:5

For his anger endureth but a moment; in his favor is life: weeping may endure for a night, but joy cometh in the morning.
Psalms 30:5

Then will I go unto the altar of God, unto God my exceeding joy: yea, upon the harp will I praise thee, O God my God.
Psalms 43:4

Joy

Thoughts of joy rise up within my spirit, concerning
God's eternal love for me. This joy, of which I
speak, like scared smoke rise quickly, into the sky,
seeking escape from a raging fire that burning out of
control, somewhere on the altar of the soul.

My joy is renewed, each time I recall Christ's
redeeming blood, that was shed on the cross,
at Calvary just to redeem me.

When I accepted Christ Jesus, as Lord and Savior
of my life and I invited the Holy Spirit to dwell
within me, I also discovered a renewable joy.

My joy is renewed with each new waking morning,
when I can accept another opportunity to experience
and share God's love with others.

In Christ, through the Holy Spirit,
the Joy of the Lord truly is my source
and my strength.

Milton Whitley, Jr.

The Invitation
An Opportunity to Obtain
Eternal Life

If you don't know Jesus Christ as your personal Savior today, I want to personally invite you to join the family of God by simply repeating (confirming) out loud with your mouth the following prayer below.

Lord Jesus, I'm a sinner, in need of a Savior. Lord forgive me of all my sin and save me. Lord Jesus I invite you to come into my heart to live, wash me clean as snow and make me a new creature. Lord Jesus, I believe that you died on the cross for me (my sins) and in three days, you rose from the dead, because you've taken the keys (the power) of death, hell, and the grave from Satan. I also believe and confess that you now sit on the right hand of the Father in Glory, making intersessions for me. Heavenly Father, I thank you for your gift of Salvation through belief in your son, Jesus. In Jesus' name I pray.

Amen

About the Author

Milton Whitley, Jr. was born on January 27, 1949 in Bakersfield, California to a very loving and hardworking family. He served in Vietnam with the 1st Marine Division. He also served in both the Army National Guard and the Air Force Reserves. Mr. Whitley attended Bakersfield College and graduated with an Associates of Arts Degree in Social Welfare. He later attended San Jose State University and received a Bachelor of Arts Degree in Social Service. Seeking further professional development, Mr. Whitley attended Fielding University where he obtained a Master of Arts Degree in Collaborative Educational Leadership. He was employed for more than 24 years with the Los Angeles County Office of Education in the Juvenile Court and Community Schools Division in Lancaster, California. Since retiring in 2010, Mr. Whitley enjoys spending time traveling, writing and being a part of various family activities. He currently resides in California City, California.